Destination:

Restoration

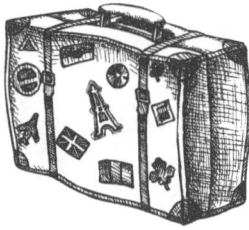

A JOURNEY PAST

ABORTION

By Karen O'Neal

ISBN 978-0-9911741-3-3

Dedicated to my husband, friend, the one I laugh with, live for, dream with, and love.

Table of Contents

My Story

From the outside, my friends and classmates thought I was the perfect kid from the picture-perfect family. But, behind the scenes, my life was anything but perfect. My dad, a professor, left my mom after twenty-three years of marriage when I was fourteen years old. He fell in love with one of his graduate students. My sisters, my mom, and I were devastated. The father I had looked up to and depended on was no longer at home.

About a year later, I started dating a boy in my youth group. I was a sophomore in high school, and he was a senior, soon to graduate. I began to look to him for support and encouragement. I thought I had found the man I was going to marry. I trusted him. My mom was busy trying to put her life back together after the divorce, so my boyfriend and I spent a lot of time together, alone. I soon gave in to my desires. I thought it was all out of love, and that made it okay. I never considered the consequences of my actions. I was seventeen years old.

Shortly after my senior year had begun, I started throwing up in the mornings and was gaining weight. My mother became concerned. So, we went for a checkup, which happened to be a doctor on the other side of town whom I had never met before. The first thing the doctor asked me was if I could be pregnant. I immediately answered, "No!"

He then asked me if I was having sex. I could not believe what was happening. I had to tell him the truth: my boyfriend and I had been sexually active for more than a year. I had never seen a gynecologist and never even thought about birth control. I was nervous and scared. I felt alone. The doctor processed a pregnancy test while my mom continued to wait in the waiting room. I got the news: I was pregnant. Without saying another word, the doctor handed me a list of abortion clinics. I left in a daze to find my mother. There was an incredible ache in the pit of my stomach. As we stood in the elevator heading to the ground floor, Mom asked me what the doctor had said. I quietly told her that I was pregnant. Her anger and embarrassment were unmistakable. The ride home was quiet.

I shared the news with my twin sister when we returned home. She was sympathetic and supportive and held me close as I cried. We heard our mom wondering aloud where she had gone wrong. I felt like I was in a horrible nightmare. My boyfriend and I were in shock. My father came over to see how I was since he knew I had a visit to the doctor, but I did not tell him what was going on. I just said I had a nervous stomach.

In the days that followed, the only solution seemed to be an abortion. There were no alternatives to consider because our family had a certain standing in the community. No one would ever know about my pregnancy, and this would all be over soon. The baby growing inside would die to maintain my family's reputation!

The procedure was scheduled the following week at a clinic on the other side of town. My boyfriend returned from school to go with us. My mom asked him to park his car in our garage so our neighbors would not see it in front of our house. We did not want word getting out to his parents or the church that he was here in the middle of the week. My mom drove us to the clinic as I sat in the back with my boyfriend. He held me the whole way. Silence filled the car.

When we arrived at the clinic, I was so afraid. I did not know what to expect. I saw a film about the upcoming procedure, but I do not remember much about it. I recall answering a few questions and signing some forms, but no one mentioned any alternatives to abortion. It was all very clinical and matter of fact. The staff referred to "the procedure," but no one ever discussed the life growing inside me. They led me to a small room. I put on a disposable gown, laid on a table with stirrups, and waited. A nurse entered to give me a shot in my hip, and then a doctor came in to examine me. He inserted something inside me to prepare me for the procedure. However, I was too far along in my pregnancy for him to complete it then – 4 ½ months pregnant. I was to come back the next day. I went home in terrible pain.

The next day we did it all over again, and this time it was for real. All I could think about was getting it behind me. I remember the horrible pain and the tugging I felt inside me. All I could hear was a loud, horrible suctioning sound. It was the most demeaning experience of my life. I squeezed the nurse's hand as the pain grew worse. And then, in a few minutes, it was over. The pump turned off, and the doctor and his nurse left the room. The room grew quiet. The life that was growing inside me was gone. I was numb. I tried not to think about what had just happened. I slept a little in the recovery room. My boyfriend went back to his classes. I felt a sense of relief. My nightmare had ended. I looked forward to getting my life back. A few days later, I returned to school. No one ever knew. Perfect.

On the surface, I went back to being president of my class and a leader in my church youth group. I told no one. I was prescribed birth control but never counseled. Deep inside, I felt shame and felt that God could not possibly want a relationship with me.

The following year, I started college at the same college my boyfriend was attending classes, but our relationship began to fall apart. I drifted from one relationship to the next, searching for love. I was in so much emotional pain, but I did not realize it. I felt so dirty. After each relationship, I was hurting more and more. Something was missing.

When I met my first husband two years later, it was different. He was accepting of my past, and we became serious and talked about a future together. We married after I graduated from college, moved to a different state, and started new jobs. We visited a few churches but never joined. It just was not a priority for either of us.

And then, seven years later, I learned I was pregnant. We were ecstatically happy! We began to search for a church. Since I was going to have a child, I decided it was time to take my faith seriously. As my pregnancy progressed, I learned a lot about the baby inside my womb. I discovered when the heart begins to beat and when the baby begins to look like a person. I began to realize the significance of what had happened in that clinic many years earlier, and I was having a tough time. I kept stuffing my feelings deep down inside me. I was full of regret and guilt about what I had done. I did not think God could ever forgive me for taking a life. God blessed us with a precious little girl. She was born healthy. Nearly two years later, our second daughter was born. I kept telling myself that God and I must be okay now. I thought if He could send me these blessings, maybe I was not so bad after all. Yet, I still felt a deep, aching sadness in my heart.

Whenever the subject of abortion came up, either in the news or just in conversation, it was difficult to hide my humiliation. I was sure everyone could see the shame of my past written all over my face.

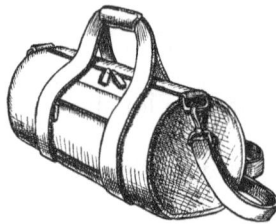

"If only you would prepare your heart and lift up your hands to him in prayer! Get rid of your sins, and leave all iniquity behind you. Then your face will brighten with innocence. You will be strong and free of fear." Job 11:13-15 NLT

Chapter 1 – Baggage Check

HANDING YOUR BAGGAGE OVER TO GOD

Abortion causes us to carry many bags. Depending on your situation and reasons for your abortion, your baggage can include guilt, shame, bitterness, anger, fear, promiscuity, addictions, grief, and low self-esteem. The bags that were heavy for me were guilt and shame. I was very embarrassed about what happened to me. I did not feel worthy of any blessings, much less having a relationship with God.

You can give each one of your bags to God, and you do not have to carry them anymore. With God's love and acceptance, you do not have to feel ashamed of your past. You do not have to be burdened by guilt about your abortion. The baby you aborted is in heaven. If you are a Christ-follower, you will someday meet your baby in heaven.

But Jesus said, "Let the children come to me. Don't stop them!
For the Kingdom of Heaven belongs to those who are like these
children." Matthew 19:14 NLT

You may not realize the grief you have for your child, but you may need to go through the same process any mother goes through to mourn their child who has died. Give your grief over to God so He may comfort you. Some women have a funeral or memorial for their aborted baby or just cry out to God for the loss of the child. Find your way to mourn your child.

God blesses those who mourn, for they will be comforted.

Matthew 5:4 NLT

When I was in my early thirties, I attended a Christian women's conference. One of the singers began to talk about her ministry. The ministry was to help in the healing process for post-abortive women. I wanted to stand up and leave as soon as she started talking about her ministry. I knew I would break down in tears if I listened to her, and I did not want the other women to know about my past. But somehow, I stayed in my seat and listened. The singer, Kathy Troccoli, spoke to women in the audience who had an abortion in their past. "Your baby is in heaven with Jesus, and you need to have a name for the baby," I remember her saying.

Wow, I thought. I had never heard anyone say this. I could not fight back the tears, and I began to sob. I could not stop. Well, it was out now, I thought. Everyone would know I had had an abortion. Kathy asked those who were hurting to come forward to pray. I have no idea how I managed to walk up to the front, but I found myself at the altar on my knees, crying, and praying. As she sang her famous song, A Baby's Prayer, I looked around, and I could not believe my eyes. I was not alone! There were other women up there, crying and praying with me. These women had experienced the same past as I had experienced, and we were all hurting. We were seeking to heal from a terrible time in our lives. We each wanted forgiveness for what we had done. As the music played, I felt cleansed as I had never felt before. It was such a relief as the years of keeping my abortion quiet came to an end. My shame was gone. I was finally able to accept God's forgiveness that I had asked for so many times before. I knew I had done something terrible, but because Jesus died on the cross for me, He forgave me. Jesus loved me despite my sins.

I named my unborn child Rose. I never knew if Rose was a girl or a boy, but I felt that she was a thorn in my side for more than 17 years, and now she was a blossoming flower, showing me how Jesus forgives us when we confess our sins to Him. The bags of guilt and shame were instantly gone!

And you must love the LORD your God with all your heart, all

your soul, and all your strength. Deuteronomy 6:5 NLT

Yes, joyful are those who live like this! Joyful indeed are those

whose God is the LORD. Psalms 144:15 NLT

Chapter 2 – Travel Companion

A RELATIONSHIP WITH GOD

When you are a Christian and get to know God's Word and pray to Him, you will start a relationship with your heavenly Father. You will learn to hear His voice through His Word, other people you meet through your journey, and through the Holy Spirit who lives within you. There is a difference between just knowing God and knowing Him intimately. When you know God intimately, you become more like Him and desire to be with Him. When you know him intimately, you will trust and love Him.

God can give you the kind of love you need. He will wrap his loving arms around you. You are not alone. Sometimes this world can be harsh, and many may turn their backs on you, but God will never turn His back on you.

Following my abortion, I felt so dirty and unworthy. I felt unloved, but mostly I did not love myself. I searched to fill the emptiness in my heart. I did not search for God but flew from God. It was not until I started going back to church (for my children) that the Holy Spirit started working on me and in me.

After the encounter at the conference and because of the lifted shame, I started sharing my story with others and began a Post Abortion Bible Study. The Bible study helped me reconnect with God. Now I have a relationship with God that I have never known before. He was there all the time, waiting for me to come home to Him. It took a long time, but I returned to His open arms. I experienced God's amazing, unconditional love through a tragedy.

As I drew closer to God my first husband didn't understand my newfound love and need for a relationship with God. He started to withdraw from me, and many times made fun of me. It was a struggle that I didn't realize I would have to deal with. I had to recognize that he just didn't comprehend the true joy I found that day at the women's conference. You may also find that your loved ones don't understand your brand-new relationship with God.

I have additionally learned to believe in God and his remarkable power. He is so much more than what I ever imagined. I tried to keep God in a box and tried to limit his abilities in my life. God is almighty and cannot fit in the box I try to put Him in. He can do the impossible in my life and your life as well. God created the universe by just speaking it into existence. Can you imagine what he can do in your life? God created you to know God and to glorify Him. He made you for a purpose, and He will help you accomplish it if you allow Him to. The answer is God! Cling to Him and rely on Him.

"For this is how God loved the world: He gave his one and only Son, so that everyone who believes in him will not perish but have eternal life." John 3:16 NLT

Jesus told him, "I am the way, the truth, and the life. No one can come to the Father except through me." John 14:6 NLT

Chapter 3 – Ticket Please

FREE TICKET TO GOD'S GRACE

God does not condemn you. He loves you, wants to save you, and accepts you as you are. God sent his Son to die on the cross to take away your sins. All you must do is receive this free ticket and believe in Jesus.

God's grace is enough no matter what you have done in life, including your abortion. Once you accept this free ticket, you can find freedom from the shame and guilt of your abortion and your past. Your slate is wiped clean, and you can start a new journey past your abortion towards eternal life.

Someday, I will see my little Rose again. I will get to hold her as my child. I know I do not deserve it. Because of God's grace and His Son, Jesus Christ, I will be with all my children one day in heaven.

You can see your aborted child(ren) in heaven. Do you believe in Jesus Christ and that He is the only Son of God who died on the cross voluntarily to cover your sins? God has given you a gift of eternal life. All you must do is believe in Jesus and accept this gift, and you will live an eternal life with God in heaven.

"If you forgive those who sin against you, your heavenly Father will forgive you. But if you refuse to forgive others, your Father will not forgive your sins." Matthew 6:14-15 NLT

Chapter 4 – Leaving the Station

LIVE AGAIN AND FORGIVE

You can leave the station by forgiving anyone you blame for your abortion: boyfriend, parent, husband, doctor, nurse, parents, etc. I blamed my mother, the doctors, my boyfriend, and the clinic counselor for my abortion. I felt that all the adults pushed me towards abortion and deceived me. I felt that I did not have any choice in the matter. It was a long time before I could forgive each of them.

Accepting God's forgiveness was the hardest thing I had to do after my abortion, and it took many years. I knew that God forgave me, but I could not accept it. I felt horrible about what I had done, and I felt like I messed up. I could not move on until I put my abortion in my past where it belonged. Satan reminds you of your past. God will show you your future and will use your past experiences for good.

I needed to use my abortion as a life lesson to help others instead of keeping my abortion stuffed in luggage stored and hidden from all. Every time I heard anyone mention abortion, I crammed the thoughts of my abortion further into my luggage. I did not want anyone to know about it. However, the day I opened that bag and placed it in front of everyone to see was the day I found God's mercy.

People who conceal their sins will not prosper, but if they confess

and turn from them, they will receive mercy.

Proverbs 28:13 NLT

I had no idea how many other women suffered the same feelings about their past abortion(s). I did not realize that others could benefit from opening that bag. What a freeing experience it was to expose my abortion and feel the love of God and not the judgment I had expected. You can also experience that same freedom by unlocking and releasing your past.

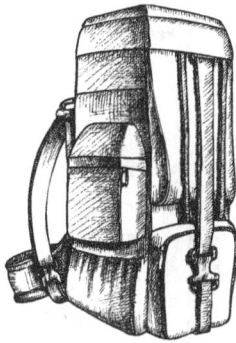

Jesus replied, "Anyone who drinks this water will soon become thirsty again. But those who drink the water I give will never be thirsty again. It becomes a fresh, bubbling spring within them, giving them eternal life." John 4:13–14 NLT

Jesus replied, "I am the bread of life. Whoever comes to me will never be hungry again. Whoever believes in me will never be thirsty." John 6:35 NLT

Chapter 5 – Dining Car

FALLING IN LOVE WITH JESUS

I love the story of Jesus talking to the Samaritan woman at Jacob's well. (John 4) She was a woman who had a past, just like you and me. She had been married five times and was currently living in sin with a man who was not her husband. However, Jesus knew of her sins even before meeting her and accepted her. He offered his living water (eternal life) to her.

Jesus accepts you and me in the same manner as he accepted the Samaritan woman. He can also give you the living water and the bread of life to sustain you through your journey. You will never be thirsty or go hungry when you believe in Jesus Christ. Is your well dry? Do you need the living water of eternal life? Recognize and follow the Lamb of God. He will cleanse you from your past.

The day I knelt on the floor at the conference, I drank from the same well the Samaritan woman drank from - Jesus' living water. Jesus immediately cleansed me from my past, and I felt a peace like I had never felt before.

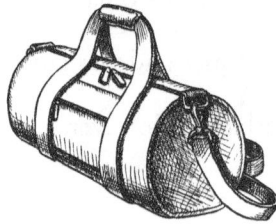

For we are God's masterpiece. He has created us anew in Christ

Jesus, so we can do the good things he planned for us long ago.

Ephesians 2:10 NLT

"For I know the plans I have for you," says the Lord. "They are

plans for good and not for disaster, to give you a future and a

hope. Jeremiah 29:11 NLT

Chapter 6 – Destination

OUR PURPOSE IN LIFE

We all must have a destination, purpose, or goal to know which way to travel. If you do not have a purpose in your life, you do not know where you are going, and you will go aimlessly down roads you were never meant to travel.

I did not think God wanted to have a relationship with me because of what I had done. So, I never sought out what God's purpose was for my life. I did what I thought I was supposed to do or what felt right or good. I learned that I must constantly lay down my selfish ways and seek God's ways. When I do this, God reveals to me my destination allowing me to travel in the right direction.

I traveled down roads I had no business traveling down in my life. Those roads were painful; divorce from my first husband, financial hardships, failed careers, etc. However, I know that God used the uneven topography to mold me and create me into the person I am today. I also know that life is not always going to be easy, smooth, or straight. God loves us enough to help us learn the lessons we need to be selfless and have a servant's heart.

"Seek the Kingdom of God above all else, and live righteously,

and he will give you everything you need." Matthew 6:33 NLT

Show me the right path, O Lord; point out the road for me to

follow. Psalms 25:4 NLT

Chapter 7 – Travel Guide

STAYING ON THE RIGHT PATH

The Bible is not only your travel guide for your journey, but the truth found in the Bible can also help heal you and bring you closer to God. The Bible is full of stories of ordinary men and women just like you and me who suffered from their past. You can learn from the stories in the Bible to better understand your Father, who loves you.

Your journey will have hills and valleys, rough roads, and storms. When you have God's Word in your heart and mind, it helps you weather the storms and pitfalls of your journey. God uses His Word and the Holy Spirit to guide you through life and help you make good decisions, as well as guide you back onto the right path when you make wrong decisions.

I highly suggest you read the Bible daily. Daily reading can help you find scriptures that the Holy Spirit will use to guide you. I have a difficult time memorizing scripture. However, the more I read and stay in the Word, the more the scriptures just come to my mind. I may not remember it word-for-word, but the basic understanding is there, and it gets me through life trials and tough decisions.

We are blessed and have such easy access to Bibles these days.

There are many translations and many formats of the Bible. Reading the Bible helps me have a better understanding of who God is. The Bible teaches us the truth and to see the wrong in our lives. It prepares us to do what God has created us to do.

The Holy Spirit is available to all believers. He lives within us and guides us in our everyday walk on this earth. The Holy Spirit not only guides us, but He has a multitude of purposes: Gives us the strength to make it each day, helps us understand the Bible, helps us worship, guides us away from wrong places, helps us pray, helps us know God's will, brings unity to believers, comforts us, etc. Allow the Holy Spirit to be your travel guide through this life showing you the truth.

And the Holy Spirit helps us in our weakness. For example, we don't know what God wants us to pray for. But the Holy Spirit prays for us with groanings that cannot be expressed in words.
Romans 8:26 NLT

When the Spirit of truth comes, he will guide you into all truth. He will not speak on his own but will tell you what he has heard. He will tell you about the future.
John 16:13 NLT

He sent out his word and healed them, snatching them from the

door of death. Psalms 107:20 NLT

Don't worry about anything; instead, pray about everything. Tell

God what you need, and thank him for all he has done.

Philippians 4:6 NLT

Chapter 8 – The Engineer

TALKING WITH GOD

Talk to God not only in times of great need during your journey but just any time you want to communicate with God. Prayer is our connection to God and the way we feel a part of Him. He already knows your needs, wants, and desires, but he likes to hear them from you.

Your prayers do not need to be said on your knees or in a well-expressed language. You can speak to God anywhere and any way you feel comfortable. God understands you. You can pray out loud or in silence. You can pray in the car or in the privacy of your bedroom. Just share your heart with God and thank Him for His blessings.

I pray quite a bit in the car. Sometimes I talk silently in my head. Other times I may shout out or cry out loud. I also communicate with God through song. I love praise and worship songs and will sing along in the car as well. When I first started my healing process with my abortion, I cried out in tears to God for forgiveness and mercy. I felt such a heavy burden to cry out. God brought me peace during these times.

Your word is a lamp to guide my feet and a light for my path.

Psalms 119:105 NLT

Chapter 9 – Arrival

CONCLUSION

I have been able to share my story several times since my abortion so many years ago. I have reconnected with God. He made it possible for me to let go of my past. I have been able to grieve for the child I lost because of a tragic choice a long time ago. All the anger I harbored for years --against my mother, my boyfriend, the doctors, and especially myself -- has lifted. Now I have a relationship with Jesus that I had never known before. I tell my friends how He was there all the time, waiting for me to come home to Him. It has taken a long time, but I returned to His open arms. I experienced God's unconditional love through a tragedy.

Through my relationship with Jesus, I was able to move on from divorce and find true love and friendship with my second husband. He has experienced the same wonderful relationship with our heavenly Father, and we live our lives as one with Him.

I pray that you will be able to arrive home and feel God's loving arms around you. I pray you will find comfort in His arms and have the knowledge that you are extraordinary to God. He loves you and wants to help you complete your journey safely.

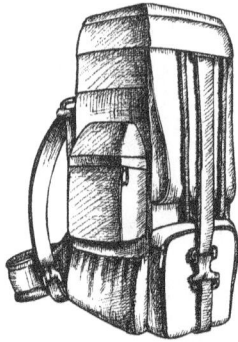

No, dear brothers and sisters, I have not achieved it, but I focus

on this one thing: Forgetting the past and looking forward to

what lies ahead, I press on to reach the end of the race and

receive the heavenly prize for which God, through Christ Jesus, is

calling us. Philippians 3:13-14 NLT

www.ingramcontent.com/pod-product-compliance
Lightning Source LLC
Chambersburg PA
CBHW071940020426

42331CB00010B/2949